MW01602617

How Socialized Health Care Will Radically Change America

-

Why Universal Health Care Will Create a Political Hegemony as In Sweden

Jon Kallberg

ISBN-13 printed edition:
978-0-9843493-0-2

ISBN-10 printed edition:
0-9843493-0-8

The publisher can be reached by email:
contact@railheadpublishing.com

RAILHEAD PRESS

WHY THIS BOOK MATTERS

This book matters because many American politicians, opinion-makers, and voters firmly believe that a public health care system would be a quick fix for what is flawed in the American health care system. In this book, I will go through the many characteristics that are unique for a public universal health care system. I will also show the impact this radical move would have on American way of life and politics. I have chosen to draw from experiences in Sweden that has one of the most comprehensive public health care systems available in the world. The Swedes' experiences with universal health care are often in sharp contrast to the promises made by the American proponents of public health care.

Issues as privacy, professionalism, abortion, parental rights, and increased taxes have not been given enough media attention. My intent with this book is to give you a broader view and increased understanding of the impact of a shift to universal health care.

Jon Kallberg

HEALTH CARE REFORM

Within the last year, health care reform has been the epicenter of the political debate. There is no doubt a need to revise and improve the American health care system. The question is what improvements or changes are needed to get better health care. It boils down to two different ideological outlooks; either a highly private system or a public system.

The initial plan from the proponents of public health care was to push a health care reform through Congress that would have been a dramatic step towards a universal health care system. The American system would then be similar to the ones that exist in countries like United Kingdom, Canada, and Sweden. That would, according to the proponents, lead to improved quality, lower the costs, enable more individuals to join, and provide coverage not only to citizens but also for illegal aliens.

During this year the debate has been intense and Congress has adjusted a few of the characteristics of the health care reform bill, but the bill is still a major shift in American life. Even if the full-blown public option did not make it through Congress, it does not mean that it is over yet with the redesigning of the American health care system. The ushers of the public health care system had of tactical reasons to slow down and they realized that they could not go the full nine yards at this attempt.

Does that mean that the issue is gone? Not at all, it will resurface under other provisions, models, structures, and organizational designs but they will have one thing in common – political influence over health care leading to a socialized health care system.

The political push to socialize American health care is here to stay. It is established as a leftist and liberal position where they want this society to turn. There has been a build up of support for public health care and this support will not go away. Strong support stems from pro-immigration groups to unions and traditional liberal groups.

If public health care was an issue in the presidential campaign of 2008, then it will return in 2012. The mechanism is there. The promise of free health care for a minority by reducing the coverage of the majority would naturally attract the vote of that minority. This works as long as the majority does not realize that they will lose services and benefits.

The main argument has been that this can be done though savings and cutting waste in the existing health care system. My argument is that it is impossible to achieve under the circumstances that we have. What I base my argument on will be revealed as you read this book.

Many of the key questions in the so called "health care reform" are still not addressed in a convincing manner like who eventually will pay, what reductions in factual service there will be for Medicare, who eventually will be entitled, and the level of freedom in the system that is assumed but not guaranteed.

The American debate about universal health care has circulated vague assumptions about what it would bring in the form of benefits – based on sketchy ideas of savings in Medicare and increased productivity to less cost in the health care sector.

These assumed system changes are based on numbers that are unlikely to be the actual fallout.

What we know is that a single payer universal healthcare system would impact society, change our moral and ethical barriers, and have a dramatic impact on the American way of life. We need only to cross-examine the way a universal health care system has impacted another country. The impact has been deep, overlapping, and changed not only the health care industry but also shaped the political landscape.

When we drill down to a lower level and study the actual transformation in ethics, fairness, justice, and responsibility towards the patient - the relevant question to ask remains, "is this the direction that the American voter anticipates?"

No American politician stands up and spells out the actual price that this extension of services would cost those who have health care today. The single payer universal health care concept is sold to the public as cheaper, more comprehensive, better, and less hassle to deal with than the system in place today. It might sound too good to be true, and it is, but a significant number of voters buy that argument at face value.

Sweden has one of the world's most comprehensive universal health care systems and has been renowned as the prototype for the welfare state that takes care of you from the cradle to the grave. I have chosen to explore the Swedish system and explain what Swedes endure to get their medical attention. A country that is embraced by liberal proponents of universal health care is a good example of how a universal health care system could be designed as the most complete "public option."

Sweden has been the ideal "nanny state" and still is in the eyes of American liberals and leftists. That has changed as Sweden has drawn conclusions from the past decades. I will explain that further in the chapter "The Swedish Concept". Today, Sweden has transformed and instead steered away from those collectivistic ideas that ruled from the 1970s to 1990s. They have learned a lesson even though many parts of Swedish society are heavily influenced by public systems and political steering instead of a working market economy.

The main Swedish health care system today is public, universal, and based on wage taxes for its funding. It is underfunded, has long waiting lists for services, and does not guarantee you, as a patient, top-notch treatment.

The question I raise is if you, as the American voter, really want this system. Apparently a majority in Congress has no issues with turning down that route as they have already started the journey. They could not secure a supermajority in the Senate if they went the full nine yards with a universal public health care system.

Because they could not get the 60 – 40 vote for a universal health care system, they had to soften the health care reform bill to be able to pass it. The push will continue. They have taken a step forward and moved to higher grounds where they can fight better. The push for universal health care is likely to be a question that is debated through this decade.

In the debate, they often use terminology such as the phrase "public option." Let me first state that these systems are not a "public option" as they will soon outmaneuver the private actors. The notion of increased competition is an illusion that serves a political purpose, as it has no bearing in reality.

The so-called competition between public and private providers is an unleveled playing field where the "public option" entities have allies in federal, state, and local government with sincere political interests of the expansion of the public entities. The politicians can easily give the public provider the upper hand by directing Medicare and Medicaid to public providers only. Therefore, the private actors will diminish over time, and it is just a matter of legislative chutzpah from the ushers of the public system and how financially able the private actors are. In the long run, the private competition will not be around if there is a universal health care system running parallel.

The combined force of these gigantic public health establishments, which comes out of the single payer universal health care system in conjunction with aligned political forces spilling over to judicial and politicized control bodies, guarantees that there will be no private viable alternatives to the average American.

Socialism and socialists hate competition. The reason is very simple. Both free market and socialism have concepts for how a society should be organized. The free market is a competing concept driven by consumers' needs in comparison with socialism that is driven by tailored political planning. Socialism, as an ideology, deeply colors both the delivery of services and the design of society itself. The vanguards of public health care that are a proponent for big government will eventually use the legislative tool to put competitors out of business and ensure that there is no functional competition or free market.

Making health care a public concern is driven from a socialist agenda that also sees free enterprises, home schooling, private wealth, and strong religious affiliations as features in America they want to limit, restrict, and try to decrease.

You don't socialize a health care system to increase competition and alternatives – you socialize the health care system because you want to kill competition and give the American people one option.

Therefore, the notion of a future of coexistence of both "public option" and free enterprises in the health care sector is a pipe dream.

The reformation of the American health care system has other, more viable ways to address the issues that are lingering. A drastic socialization of the health care system would lead to further decline in service quality and less service for more money for the average American. It would also increase the tax burden and slow down economic recovery because people would have to pay higher taxes and have less money to spend on buying services , which in turn decreases revenues for businesses.

I repeat again to put more emphasis on the fact: for any socialist a free market and free enterprises are a competing model for production and services that contradict the socialistic concept of public governance and publicly owned means of production and services. Free market liberates the individual to make their own choices – in a socialist world the government and your political overhead will make these choices for you. America has never been and never will be a country where you are told that you have only one option; it is anti-American, in direct opposition to the American way of life.

The sentiment of urgency to hastily create a new system makes it easier to do radical changes. It is one of the oldest political tricks – the creation of the mutual feeling of urgent crisis. We have had a housing crisis, we now have a health care crisis, and we have a global warming crisis. The voters could step out of the normal boundaries, as will moderate politicians, if the sentiment of crisis becomes accepted.

The American health care system has had serious flaws for the last decades because it assumed that everyone has a job and the employer pays for health care. Add to that other assumptions that are not realistic in today's world. Time has made parts of the American health care system obsolete. Can it be fixed quickly by tearing the whole system down and replacing it with a completely different system by copying how it is done in other countries? First, we must recognize the obvious: what is a fit for other countries might not be fit for America as there are significant differences between the countries.

I will return to these differences but just to give you an early hint I will quickly display a few. European countries have, in many cases, impeccable population registries that determine who is eligible or not. The only identification we actually could trust in America is the U.S. passport. That is the only identification where we can assume that the holder is a legal resident and appearing under his or her legal name.

If the American universal health care system does not verify eligibility it would lead to anyone wanting "free" health care could just walk in and demand it. That opens the floodgates for fraud, free riding, and an unprecedented spike in costs.

Another example is the fact that over a fifth of all Americans pay no taxes. In Europe almost all adults pay taxes. That means that even low income families in Europe contribute to the universal health care system meanwhile the same system in America would have a tremendous level of free riding. The costs for American health care would be carried by only a part of the population but everyone would have access – including the estimated 12 million illegal immigrants that work in the "off the books" economy.

These fundamental differences undermine the argument that America can adopt a universal healthcare system like Sweden, France, or any other developed European state. That is just the basics – if their system is applicable on American society.

That is even before raising any questions about the moral and societal fitness for a universal health care system in America. A single payer universal health care system is a foreign concept and runs counter to American traditional values.

POLITICALLY MANAGED HEALTH CARE - DO YOU WANT IT?

By being born Swedish and having had a long exposure to the government-run universal health care, I would like to add a few hidden tenets that come with the stepwise governmental take over of health care - and the gigantic governmental agency that follows.

The idea of universal health care sounds really good. It is hard to resist, the free for all universal health care administered by the government, financed by stunning slashes by cost cutting, and improved efficiency within the health care system. It would be an easy sell - if it was true. I want to draw your attention to the unaddressed effects of universal health care, and the role of these new entities and how they would affect our daily lives.

Political power does not come in a decree or shouted out by a herald – it comes in the fine print when it becomes criteria for services and expected health care.

Repeatedly has the word "redistribution" surfaced in the health care reform debate as "fair and moral," as seen from the proponents' usage of American economic power to provide universal health care.

The power to set the criteria that comes with the stewardship of these health care entities and also political power over the legislative arm can be used to create socio-economic change and "redistribution." The wording "redistribution" runs like a red thread through the demagogic, broad speeches that favors a nationalized health care.

The concept of redistribution is well established in the socialist world. It was one of Che Guevara's favorite words and still is a permanent fixture in Fidel Castro's vocabulary. It simply means that someone will decide if you will get your money's worth of services that you paid for or if they will give it to someone else based on their political preferences.

Redistribution is to take from some citizens and give to others based on a political agenda. If you do it privately by just taking stuff from people to give to others that you really like, you go to jail. In a world where everything is negotiable, it does not put you in jail as long as it serves the political goal of redistribution. Instead taking from one group to give to another is considered a good deed for a socialist. It is considered "moral." The morality is that you should not have your money's worth of what you paid for because you had the opportunity, worked hard, or were fortunate to play your cards in the right order. You do not deserve what belongs to you; it has to be shared with those whom the government favors. Even Rousseau said that morality is a human construct and it is negotiable – the question is if you want to depend on a political system or health care system that has the same outlook.

Redistribution makes the "Cold War" look like a pointless exercise as socialism is put into play in America and starts to steer how we honor the rights of every citizen to his or hers equity, money, and ultimately in health care, life, and happiness.

Medicine and health care is power. It is the power over our lives and it impacts us no matter how we try to distance ourselves. We need health care at different points during our lives and the controller of these resources makes decisions that will either harm or benefit you. In the worst case scenario they might kill you, maybe not intentionally, but it becomes a life and death issue when you no longer meet their preferred criteria to receive the top of the line treatment. You might instead be offered less modern or less professional treatment as a way of saving money. Nationalized health care will always be cash strapped as it is obligated to provide some health care for everyone. But, since it is based on taxation, there are limits to how much they can raise taxes.

Today, the American health care industry represents about 16% of GDP. That will be lower with universal health care but not as a saving per se because the order of priorities would change. In reality, elderly and already critically sick individuals would get less of the top notch and expensive treatments as the government does not see it as a sound investment. They do not have any productivity left to pay back the government in taxes over the next years. It is a pure expense for the government. The government will put its own interest first as they are provider, payer, decider, and legislator.

Another major difference is the reduction of preventive care as universal health care systems are reactive instead of proactive. Services are provided once you are unhealthy and sick instead of promoting wellness through preventive care. Universal health care is also heavily reliant on providing services by staff and not by external, independent service providers. That means in real terms that psychologists, as an example, that are traditionally independent providers would be replaced by governmental staff psychologists. Your options to choose a therapist would be limited if not nil. It does not matter if you dislike or do not trust the therapist; this is what is provided, end of story.

There is no need for patient consideration unless it is so upsetting that it carries severe political consequences. Once the government sets the agenda, it would be very hard to change as it becomes state or national standards. In a system that caters to everyone from the same pool of resources there will naturally be competition for resources. The losers in that competition will be the ones with very limited political voice like the elderly, unborn children, and disabled.

But what would universal health care be like? It is a complex question to answer but the key word to start with would be "pooling". The idea is that resources are put into a pool and then, by political stewardship, distributed according to the needs of the care seekers.

Let us use an example for pooling. The word "pooling" is frequently used to describe how money could be saved if we had a public health care system. The concept of pooling is simple. Instead of each of us having our own money, we put all our money in one basket as a group and someone decides how it is utilized. Already we should see a red flag.

So, let us talk about pooling with an example. In a workplace ten people earn $2,000 that they carry home every month. Instead of everyone walking home with $2,000, let us run this according to the principles of public health care. We will pool the $2,000 and there will be a pool of resources of $20,000 with ten participants. That should cover all ten peoples' living expenses based on the decisions of one person out of these ten. The decision maker will be able to keep for themselves the money that is not paid out of the total pool of $20,000. The decision maker in this example represents the political establishment and the government in a public health care system.

Instantly we understand that the 10th person who is the decision maker will start to cut the payments to the others to be able to increase the surplus.

Universal health care is no democracy. It is a political construct that will pay from the common pool based on decisions of a political elite and money that is not spent is funneled back to the government and can be spent on their own pet projects of feeding an entitlement program to buy voting power. In government there is always a competing alternative for usage of funds. The decision maker will foot your bills from the $20,000 but you will not get the $2,000 that is your share. The government has other plans for the surplus.

Can you pick a fight and get your $2,000 share in any other way? Probably not because you do not have the political clout to break through and change or challenge the system – especially since politicians could use surpluses from others to feed the entitlement programs to solidify their political power.

You will be locked in and forced to accept less than you paid into the pool and you do not have the political leverage to change that fact.

Have you, by giving up your right to individual health care, funded a mammoth organization that will spearhead a leftist hegemony? You bet.

I would like to go back to the example with going from having $2,000 in your wallet to having a share in a $20,000 pool of resources. In the example, I used living expenses and we know what they are: gas, dwelling, food, electricity, and necessary costs of living. These are due immediately and can not be delayed as it would lead to loss of service or utility. So, if you are only provided $1,450 from the $20,000 pool, the manager is able to divert $550 into their other projects that actually belonged to you. The loss of this $550 would be a significant reduction of your standard of living and it would be obvious. You can check how much you lost and it is transparent. You would know how much had been taken from you and you could critique the system as being unfair. It is so blatant when you walk into your home and there is no electricity or water and those who managed the $20,000 have not paid your bills.

When a pool is small it is transparent and you will be able to understand what you paid and what you got. A huge universal health care system would lack that transparency because it would no longer be visible due to size, complexity, and nature of services rendered.

Let's now instead turn this $20,000 pool of resources to a real universal health care pool. First you will not be 10 members chipping in $2,000. You will be as an example one of the 1,000,000 members paying $2,000 meanwhile another 1,000,000 members pay nothing. The universal health care pool will then use the same guidelines for both the paying and the non-paying members. At this starting point, you have lost half your paid in health care benefits due to involuntary sharing.

So you pay $2,000 to get $1,000 coverage, but it would not be as transparent as the first example because of the size of this pool makes it hard to get an overview and to translate that to your own received good. That is the political beauty of it. The system is set up in a way that it is almost impossible for you to get a sense of the real value of the money you pour in.

We are not done with our example yet. So you pay $2,000 for the $1,000 health care benefit as in the example above but what is really delivered? Will you get the full value of these $1,000 health care benefits as soon as you need them? No, the resources are not there. The $1,000 benefit is a theoretical number and the actual is far less because the typical features of a universal health care system includes waiting lists and queuing for services.

What is a waiting list? In real terms, a waiting list is a delayed delivery with a higher demand for the good than can be delivered. Your argument would then be that you already paid double into the system to get it so it owes the service to you. True, and they admit that by putting you on the waiting list. So you have the right to $1,000 worth of benefit, but it will not be delivered when you need it.   Waiting lists are the government taking up a credit by using your health as the risk. If they do not need to deliver the service at the same moment you need it, that means that they do not have to pay – as they are payer and provider.

So the government can charge you $2,000 for health care by taxation, give $1,000 to buy the vote from someone else who not be paying taxes by providing "free" care and then just provide the lowest level of service like local clinics and put you on the waiting list for what is expensive. In real terms the value of that $2,000 you poured into the system is now down to a few hundred dollars.

After eight, ten or twelve months you will get the operation you waited for with the risk of worsened conditions or fatality. The government does not really care because they were able to borrow cheap money and provide less care and capacity than the taxes they collected.

If universal single payer health care was a service offered by any other provider, it would be classified as consumer fraud but when provided by government it will be mandatory. So, who will end up on the waiting list and not get their services as soon as possible?

The key word is criteria – which is politically defined but other factors could have an impact. Other factors can include budget constrains, which means that government prefers to spend the money somewhere else, by a doctor's decision or driven by policies from the government entity that provides the universal health care. Does that mean that you have the right to get the care you need? No, not at all. It is all up to this mammoth entity to decide.

The easiest way for the government to quickly save money is to delay the payout of services and deny any advanced medical procedure based on your productive life cycle. If you are elderly – then you are out.

For those who grew up within these health care systems they have nothing to compare with and naturally they might have concerns about the American system as it is today. The American health care system has several issues that have to be addressed, but you do not fix a broken system by switching to another broken system.

In the European universal health care systems, the fees are tied directly to your income. That makes the "redistribution" even higher to others as you start to pay a substantial part of your income to fund other peoples' health care.

The fairness in the system is lost when it is taken from your income with no correlation to your age, health, risk, or any other health related factor. Therefore, it is wrong to call universal health care "health insurance for everyone" because it is not insurance. It is a tax.

Insurance is a price you pay for coverage that is directly linked to the risk and probability that you would actually use the services offered. If you are often sick or have a chronic health condition you pay more for health insurance, as it is likely that you will utilize the services.

There is a direct link between you, your risks, and what you pay. In universal health care there is absolutely no link between these factors at all.

You can never expect to get the health care services you pay for as it is just a contribution to a pool of resources that is open for anyone to tap into without any real contribution. So what happens when you really need access to health care because you have a severe illness and cannot afford to wait on the waiting list for months? You end up paying for health care services a second time.

What does this mean in practical terms? Let me give you an example from my own life.

Almost twenty years ago when I lived in Sweden, I damaged my right knee after I fell. My children were young, I was the sole breadwinner in the family, and I had my own business. That year and in years prior, I had paid substantial amounts of money in health care tax. This was the time for me to get my money's worth of services.

I was in urgent need of surgery. As a business owner I had to get back to work as soon as possible to be able to maintain my business, provide for my family, and meet the expectations of my customers in order to keep them. The answer from the universal health care system was stunning. There was no way I could get a simple knee surgery for at least eight months according to the waiting list. What made it even worse was that these eight months were not carved in stone and it could turn out to even take ten or twelve months before I could get my treatment. So what were my options at that time? None.

There was no way I could survive financially paying for a house, family, and continue my business from only short term disability payouts for eight to ten months. I had to take actions – and these actions were because I never had any health coverage or health care benefits. Even though I had paid taxes for several years to pay for my universal health care, it was not there for me when I needed it.

I ended up paying $10,000 at a private facility to get my knee taken care of and it was done within a month so I could start working again in less than two months after the accident.

Could I afford it? I had to – even if I eventually borrowed the money from my parents.

In my case there was no option to do it any other way and this is the reality with universal health care. Those Americans who can not afford to be away from their jobs or businesses for six or ten months will, in a universal health care system, face the same choice – either buy it with cash because you never had health care coverage or face that your personal finances are laid to ruin.

Researchers have documented that the waiting list for a knee surgery in Sweden during that specific time was between 6 months to 24 months. That means in plain English that it could have taken me up to two years before my knee surgery would have been provided even though I had already paid for it through taxes.

If you are a business owner, taking care of loved ones, or for any other reason need to be quickly back in play after an accident or injury you will, in a universal health care system, face the choice of either pay out of pocket to get the treatment you need or take the risk of ruining your life and others by waiting for months on a waiting list.

A universal health care system is prone to be underfinanced, as they all are all over the world, and that means in real terms that there will be no advanced health care services provided when you actually need them. In the best case scenario you are put on a waiting list.

It is a natural and human reaction that we want good health care and also health coverage for the uninsured without raising the cost for anyone. The only hurdle is that it can not be done. It would be wizardry – someone will end up paying. The sums do not match up. At the end someone has to pick up the bill. If the government can not pay for the uninsured without raising taxes, there are only three options left – decrease the level of health care provided for existing insured, raise taxes to pay for the uninsured, or, as government often prefers to do, both of them.

The challenges American health care faces does not have quick solutions and many avenues could be tested within the existing system like allowing competition across state lines, tort reform, limiting the ways prescription drugs are marketed, fighting corruption, and fraud. One avenue is not the solution and many of these options might not be viable or will be in conflict with other more important values. There is no silver bullet.

The quick fix of converting, in a stepwise way, the American health care system to a single payer universal health care system would be extremely unwise as it would create an underfunded mammoth that will provide subpar services that are diluted within the population so those who today have health insurance will be paying double – first for the public services through taxes and then to actually get coverage by buying it private.

When America starts on the road called "public option," these created public health care entities will maneuver together with their ushers to expand their realm of interest – and the way is paved for a nationalized health care system as in socialist countries. If the "public option" fails to be competitive, the public health care entities will have the support of politicians that with the rule of law eventually transfer a larger part of the health care sector to the "public option".

In socialized health care there is no connection between what you pay and what you get. The American economy was formed on the idea that you pay and you get what you pay for. A system that takes your money without committing to deliver anything in real terms and then puts it up to their discretion to give you anything back is foreign to the American mindset.

A nationalized health care system is not the quick fix that its proponents claim. It is a vehicle for long-term political and economical influence and will change America in a more radical way than we can portray today.

PLAN B

In this book, I, as an author, have intentionally avoided going into too much details of the different plans for government run health care and instead focused on the mere principles, overlaying rules, and political mechanism that would have an influx. The plans that have been presented have changed form and varied in the amount of tax money sought; one of which is the organizational form, but they all follow the same concept. The "public option" as a concept is clear.

It will be a large public system that will, in the long run, replace the existing health care system as we know it today.

Even if they stop at "Plan B" or eventually "Plan C" for now we know that they are aiming for "Plan A" – the nationalized single payer universal health care system.

The "Plan B," as news media refers to it, is the remaking of the "public option" to instead be private, non for profit organizations that will be initially funded by the government. It will, in theory, start to compete with the existing health care industry and, again in theory, by cost savings and pooling create an abundance of resources to share with those who are not covered by health care.

The so called "Plan B" sounds really good: the government only needs to provide the seed money.

A few billion dollars of taxpayer money to these non for profits, and then the issue will be solved and we have a so called "public option."

What "Plan B" is really saying is let us take billions of tax money, buy ourselves a marketplace for our non for profits by buying out private health care providers. Then we create non for profit private entities with no transparency, because they are now non-governmental, and then fill these non for profit entities with the people that initially were proponents for universal health care.

These non for profit entities created in "Plan B" are embryos of the universal, nationalized, socialist health care. The ushers of the public health care do not have the political clout to pull it through to its full extent so they have to settle for less for now.

The non for profit health care organizations that are created will have political ties to those politicians that usher universal health care. They will have access to taxpayers' money through public funding, which we can assume will be greater than the initiation because they would need money to organize and reform. As they are a non for profit and a private entity, there still would not be transparency for the taxpayers.

If they are non for profit organizations, they enjoy better protection from any outside information seeker, journalist, or regular citizen who tries to find out what is going on than do large, private enterprises.

The large companies have to open up their books for many reasons, especially for federal regulators and the governance of the stock markets. A non for profit organization can be as secretive as the Church of Scientology is with what they decide – and still they will have billions of tax dollars rolling in to be seed money for a "public option." A non for profit organization is primarily responsible and accountable towards their board and charter. If the charter supports secretive behavior, and the board has to follow the charter, then you will actually watch billions disappear in a black hole if they are funded.

Think about it. Which nominees will be on the board for these organizations? Who will nominate them?

The ushers of the socialist health care system will nominate their own loyalists to these entities as they are cadre organizations for the next step – the socialist health care system. The "Plan B" is a secure way to ensure that the nationalization of American health care can start and grow with taxpayer money.

There will be no new hospitals built for these non for profit organizations. So, the new entities have two options. Either acquire assets from private enterprises or through unfair competition spearheaded by the politicians' maneuver to put the private enterprises out of business.

One of the most relevant discussions surrounding the so called "Plan B" private non for profits has not started. The question is what should be done if they financially fail?

Maybe, I say maybe, the private health care companies and providers are already equipped to deliver health care and if these new non for profits are going to live under the same economical stars as any of their competitors, but what makes them able to survive in the fierce competition?

Or is it staged so they will need public funding in the long run which would drive the government deeper and deeper into the health care sector and pave the way for the socialized universal health care system?

So, would financially failing non for profit health care organizations be a Trojan horse for nationalized health care? The final outcome could actually be as simple as that. Once the government has sunk billions of dollars into these entities, the government would likely refuse to shut them down when they fail due to the large investment financially and ideologically. The non for profits can not survive by themselves, and then government does a takeover. Suddenly we have socialized health care.

The introduction of socialized health care can come with failing non for profits a few years down the road. It is then no longer the introduction of nationalized health care. It will then be tailored as a "financial rescue to ensure health care" when the federal government enters the arena as health care provider.

If a non for profit could provide cheaper health care for more people by just being a non for profit, we could start one right now – you, me, and a few more readers. The problem is if our non for profit would be financially successful even with governmental seed funding. Still there are many actors out there who have paid off facilities, lean organizations, and actually know what they are doing.

Our, sad to tell you, non for profit is unlikely to last so long. Non for profits are, by creation, not predestined to outcompete any other provider. These non for profits will live and exist in the same economy as others in the health care market.

For these non for profits to survive financially they would need political power to get rid of competition and a never ending flow of tax money to ensure their growth, stability, and ability to deliver health care. So we have nationalized health care in another form.

The case for "Plan B" is that by creating lower costs and putting pressure on others to deliver at lower costs – and by doing so create a general saving. That requires four assumptions, first that the "Plan B" non for profit organizations are not marginal actors in the market. They have to be very dominant; otherwise, they would have no impact on pricing in the market.

The second assumption is that there are actually huge cost savings to be made and that the waste in the health care industry is so large that only the non for profits are able to get a grip on the waste. That requires that the waste and the possible cost savings are significant, up to a third of the overall budget.

Unless the non for profit pays their nurses a third less, their doctors a third less, uses a third less of energy in their buildings, and builds a facility a third cheaper than everyone else, which is just a pipe dream, quality in care would fall dramatically or it would need additional funding from taxpayers.

Large organizations are lucky if they can run operations a few percentages cheaper than their competitors. The "Plan B" non for profit entities that Congress envisions are preset to either fail or become a long term taxpayer burden. The third assumption is that these entities will be up and running as functional providers from day one. This does not take into consideration that these entities are created from scratch with no facilities or staff.

The fourth assumption goes with the second to the degree that the cost savings are so significant that we can provide services for maybe a fourth or a third more patients that before were uninsured and we can do that without lowering the quality, asking the government for more tax money, or raising the actual out of pocket expense for the patients.

Let us go back to starting an organization from scratch as mentioned in the third assumption. Totally ignored is that there are significant structural, transactional, and organizational costs of designing a completely new set of actors in the market as the "Plan B" non for profits will be. They need offices, facilities, newly trained staff, and capacity to serve, adjust, construct, and remodel facilities.

To start organizations from scratch is very costly; especially if they are large and dealing with complex matters. So, the initial cost for the government to initiate these "Plan B" entities will be substantial without their ability to deliver any public good in the form of health care.

So, we will divert billions of dollars just to get their offices up and running, money that otherwise could have been in play in the private economy as money never taxed from the citizenry, or been spent in Medicare or other existing programs and that already generate health care goods.

The "Plan B" is, to a degree, even worse than socialized health care because it takes the taxpayers' dollars and does not offer the transparency we have in a direct run governmental program, or show any tangible cost savings.

In governmental programs, we have a legal accountability towards the taxpayers, the oversight from GAO, inquiries from the political opposition, and ways for investigative journalists to find the truth through the Freedom of Information Act – all these safeguards are gone with the non for profits.

THE SWEDISH CONCEPT

The Swedish health care system is organized by eighteen county councils and two regions that each cover between three hundred thousand and million inhabitants. The historical origin is the county council called *Landsting* that was initially created several hundred years ago as administrative entity.

The word *Landsting* is over thousand years old and is directly translated "the decision making gathering in a province" and served as a middle layer between villages and hamlets on one side and the royal national administration on the other side. From the 17th century it was taken over by the state and the royal administration as it tightened its grip over provinces. From the year 1862 it was given the form of a municipal union to supervise and collect taxes for roads, bridges, and necessary infrastructure.

As the need for health care increased in Sweden during the 19th century, the *Landsting* started to engage in being a health care provider at a marginal level. The first expansion of public health care in Sweden occurred between the 1920s and1950s when it becomes the predominant provider. As the socialists are able to gain influence over politics, they identify the importance of politically controlled health care. The era of Labor Party stewardship in government between the 1920s up until the 1980s is a never ending expansion of the *Landsting*. In the 1970s, the *Landsting* got more involved in rehabilitation, drug abuse prevention, culture, financing regional theaters, symphony orchestras, dance groups, disabled workers rehabilitation, immigrant's integration, and other fields related to societal issues.

It, to a degree, became a "slush account" for pet projects for leftists as the transparency and actual procurement processes were less tedious in the county councils than in the national government. These pet projects were funded by utilizing funds received for the health tax by extending the already extensive interpretation of the *Landsting* charter.

What started as a way to fund infrastructure in the 1800s became a health care provider using taxation to pay for universal health care and then transformed to a leftist political power house with tentacles that spread all over the civic society.

Is it a given that these entities will be leftist vehicles for influence? Yes, and it is naturally linked to its creation. It is a public entity that provides subpar services at high expense. Already we realize that a conservative and fiscally responsible citizenry is a direct threat to this organization. The mammoth health care entities do not want to be responsible towards the people, they want to overtax for less services rendered, and they prefer politicians that are big spenders.

The *Landsting* themselves are big government and happy spenders of other people's money. Governmental agencies want to expand their realm of influence and the Swedish county councils, *Landsting*, have been formidable players in that field.

The universal health care system became law in 1946, but it took ten years before it could be implemented because it was underfunded when the law was passed. It wasn't until the middle of the 1950s that the state tried to live up to its obligations. Since the 1960s, Sweden has had a completely universal health care system paid for by tax money. The era of a public choice lasted to the mid 1990s when doctors started to see a business opportunity in the failing ability to provide care by the public health care system standards.

From the mid 1990s Sweden has had a move towards private health care as a compliment to the general universal health care system. It started as private clinics and surgeons catering to clients paying out of pocket who were paying cash to avoid long waiting lists and subpar health care.

In the early 2000s, private companies started to offer outsourcing of health care from the public entity because a private, fast moving market oriented free enterprise can do more for less than a huge public health care provider. The private Swedish health care providers have grown step by step and are today a significant part of the Swedish health care system. So the American intended public health care would go in completely the opposite direction – from market economy to socialism. Sweden has learned that lesson and is now slowly moving back to free enterprises instead of public entities.

Once health care is nationalized, there needs to be integration with pharmacies and the wholesale of drugs as there is only one major buyer. So pharmacies and drug wholesalers become nationalized. The Swedes nationalized pharmacies and drug wholesale in 1970. This created *Apoteksbolaget*, the public pharmacy company that had a complete monopoly of pharmaceutical sales and wholesale. The reason was very simple. The private pharmacies stood in the way of the big health care entity, so political pressure came from the left and the nationalized health care system to also nationalize the drug trade because it would be "rational" according to the proponents. When you start the journey to nationalize it continues as the nationalized entities require more territory and wants to fend off any competition. In 2010 the privatization of former public pharmacies began and they will be sold out to pharmacists and drug companies during the course of the upcoming years. Almost 40 years later, the Swedes realized that it does not work to nationalize.

So the Swedes have gone a long way from the so called "welfare state" that many Democrats in Congress favor. Swedes have started to privatize their pension system, they privatize pharmacies, Swedish children can pick any school they want as they receive a school check, lower corporate taxes, and health care is becoming more operated by free enterprises in a market economy environment. The Sweden that these pro-nanny state Democrats envisioned no longer exists. It failed in the 1980s and 1990s and Sweden is moving away from these ideas. Sweden is moving towards increasing free enterprise, lowering taxes, and welcoming open and fair competition. Today America is doing the opposite.

The Swedish system has guaranteed citizens and permanent residents basic health care services at a low direct outlay and subsidized prescribed drugs also sold at a low cost. This has been financed by taxes for employed and self-employed by adding an additional tax to the *landsting* 13% to their tax bracket. The *landsting* is the regional health care provider and is legally an association of municipalities in a specific region. If you had a tax bracket before of 40%, you now suddenly had 53% as a tax bracket. The tax to the *landsting* is in reality a health care tax.

The weakness with this system is that it is all based on salaries – but the Swedes have addressed this differently through the last thirty years aggressively with audits, tax inspectors, and other legal actions enforced tax laws to their fullest extent and brought down the informal sector to a fraction of that in America. It is fiscally impossible to have a tax based system without very aggressive tax enforcement.

The Swedes have an advantage compared to America in determining who is eligible in their public health care system – they have an almost bullet proof population registry that quickly determines citizen status and the authorities share information in ways that would be illegal in the United States. Swedish police can, without probable cause, pull any driver over and out of the blue run a citizen status check on the driver. The concept of probable cause does not exist. That makes it far harder for illegal immigrants to live in Sweden compared to the United States and illegal immigrants are denied many social services including universal health care.

Sweden allows illegal immigrants to legalize their status but a vast majority are deported. That active strategy of deportation differs from the United States.

The United States has two major hurdles for successful implementation of the universal health care compared to Sweden – in the United States there is an issue with about ten to fifteen million illegal immigrants that are uncovered by health insurance and their eligibility has to be determined and the size of the unofficial "off the books" economy.

The lack of a bullet proof population registry that easily can determine status of each individual at a federal level would also create a high degree of uncertainty of who is fully eligible for the health care coverage in United States if the system would be universal and federal. If we do not know who is eligible or if there are ways to trespass the system, we can assume that fraud in the system would be rampant.

So even if the United States had the money or if the taxpayers would gladly pay the additional taxes to ensure that as many as possible got health care through a universal health care system, there are significant differences that would make it harder and more prone to failure to implement in the United States. The only way to ensure success would require fundamental changes in the relationship between citizen and government, where the American citizenry would have to accept that government would prevail in any conflict of interests. The public interest has the right of way. A shift that puts Americans back where they once started – as loyal servants to King George III in its modern shape.

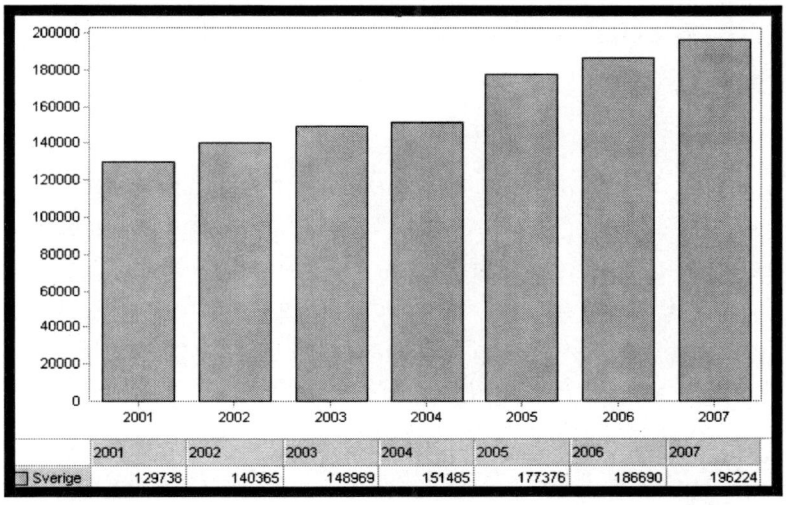

	2001	2002	2003	2004	2005	2006	2007
Sverige	129738	140365	148969	151485	177376	186690	196224

One of the most emphasized arguments for the implementation of universal health care in America is the growing cost for health care. The argument also includes assumptions on the ability for universal health care systems to be able to control this increase. The Swedish health care system has had a cost increase of 51% between 2001 and 2007. As of the year 2007, the cost increases in the Swedish system and the American system as it is per today is almost at the same level – 5 to 6% per annum. Universal health care does not have a systematic advantage when it comes to cost control. Data source: The Swedish County Council and Municipalities Association.

As the government in Sweden calls the shots, it can also determine when and how Swedes get their health care in the universal health care system. To cut costs, the system relies heavily on out-patient care and tries aggressively to cut hospital in-patient days. The Swedish average for hospitalization in general is 6 days, by an international level a low figure, and the dependency on out-patient services are taken to a level that will compromise the patient's care.

When you decrease the number of hospitalization days and discharge patients earlier, there are significant cost savings – but also a dramatically increased risk that is transferred to the patient without their informed consent or their being given any other option. In a universal health care system you are discharged, so even if you want to pay with your own money to stay, you will be discharged with minimal consideration for how you actually feel or what pain you suffer.

It is technically based on a doctor's assessment of you, but this assessment is heavily influenced by non-medical factors such as if there is a shortage of hospital beds at that very moment, if they are running over budget, and if they need to meet statistical goals. Their reasoning is administrative and not based on your actual needs.

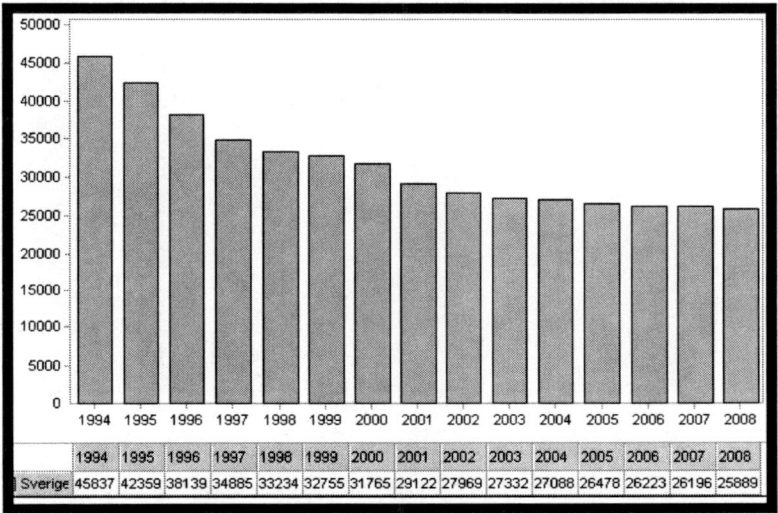

	1994	1995	1996	1997	1998	1999	2000	2001	2002	2003	2004	2005	2006	2007	2008
Sverige	45837	42359	38139	34885	33234	32755	31765	29122	27969	27332	27088	26478	26223	26196	25889

Sweden has decreased the total number of hospital beds for in-patient care so only 56% of the hospital beds available in 1994 exist in 2008. The universal health care system saves money for the government by refusing you proper care and, instead, increasing waiting lists. Data source: The Swedish County Council and Municipalities Association.

The risk they take if they discharge you prematurely is marginal as the universal health care system is protected from law suits and transfer the complaints to a complaint board. It might reprimand the doctor and "compensate" the injured person with amounts that are more pennies than dollars.

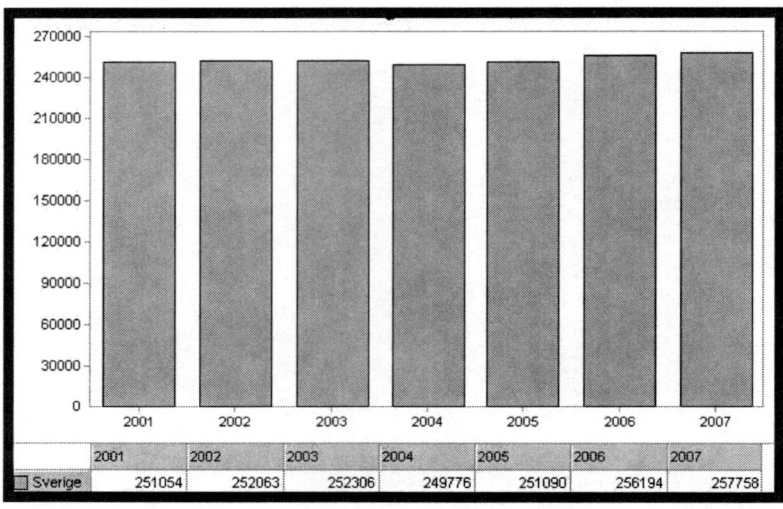

	2001	2002	2003	2004	2005	2006	2007
Sverige	251054	252063	252306	249776	251090	256194	257758

So if hospital beds are dwindling and patients are discharged at an unprecedented rate from the hospitals to save money for the Swedish universal health care system, would there not be any staff cuts? Not at all, instead the hired staff has slightly increased. The reason is simple; health care worker unions are more powerful than patients in a socialized health care system. Data source: The Swedish County Council and Municipalities Association.

In Sweden, I had a 2nd knee operation that was a minimally invasive procedure. This time I did it at a government run hospital as a part of the universal health care system. I was discharged the same moment I could barely stand up and talk to a doctor in the recovery room after anesthesia. There was no real checking of my condition or the actual stitching of the surgical cut. I walked down to the entrance to get a cab to take me home, and, as I walked down the hallway to the reception area, the stitches opens up and blood stained my jeans like I have been shot in the leg. I fell on the floor and, after some confusion; I ended up at the ward where I was discharged. Even in a third world country you would be admitted to stay the night to recover, get new stitches, and clean up after all the blood but this was a first world country with government run health care. They discharged me again after I got new stitches, with bloodied jeans, and I had to give them one credit. They called a cab that waited downstairs when I did my second attempt to leave the building.

There is no way that I successfully would be able to win a claim against the hospital. It was an accident. It does not matter that I was staged for the accident because nobody really checked my stitches. Your rights as a patient are taken away from you and there is no way for you to get heard.

The personal experience of a health care system like this has one big asset – it is a personal experience. The proponents of universal health care in America have a few valid arguments – the number of uninsured, social equality, the dependency of financial resources to get premium health care, and the link between employment and benefits.

Many of these challenges can be addressed in other ways than creating a government run health care system that will be stretched to the limits and deliver mediocre care at a very high price. It is not fair to highly tax citizens with the promise of health care and then fail to deliver when needed.

That also undermines other things that come with citizen's notion of paying taxes without getting anything in return – increased unofficial economy and tax avoidance. Any person that feels that they are paying for something that is not worth it will react. If a large fraction in America do not pay taxes nor can be determined with legal precision as eligible in a universal health care system, it will catalyze a weakened tax loyalty within those groups that actually pays for the others.

FOLKHEMMET

In the early 1920s, Sweden started to develop a collectivistic concept called *Folkhemmet*, the home of the people, with the analogy of a society as a home for all and that the policies that followed should cater to everyone's needs. It is a socialist concept that believes firmly in the politically designed society. The government will meet your needs.

"From each according to his ability, to each according to his need"

Karl Marx 1875

The concept of the right to redistribute from whatever surplus there is by one person and give it to whom the political power believes has the need is key to any Marxist communism or socialism. Therefore, the socialized medicine is an ideal picture of socialism at work.

A single payer universal health care is a pivotal component in a socialist design of a society. Once you depend on the government for your health care, you actually are at their mercy. It might sound harsh, but it is true. If government determines if you get treatment, medicine, and access to hospitals, you would take in to consideration the interests of the government, since it guarantees your health care. It might not be conscious but you cannot ignore it.

A government that takes a large share of your resources has a vested interest that you are productive as a taxpayer and that you cannot cheat on taxes because it is their source of income and any "off the books" business would be a serious offense against the government as the game has been turned. The government no longer serves you; you are now serving the government.

Once that game has changed, people are dispensable. They are production resources for the government like electricity, plumbing, and sheet metal. The citizens are no longer a threat, through tax revolts, revolution, or their vote, to the government as entitlements tie enough votes to ensure electoral victory for the ruling regime.

If you ensure a minority the right to financially live off another hard working majority and you put a huge stack of dependent governmental employees – then you have created the "democratic" dictatorship. It is a political system that has no incentive to change because, at the end of every election, government employees and those entitled to live off others productivity will eventually make up the 51% necessary to control the society.

Folkhemmet, as a concept, is what many American leftists would like to see: the society that covers all aspects of life and where your daily life is heavily dependent on political and not individual decisions.

It has all the components of a pseudo-dictatorship:

- High taxes because the government now provides the services you used to buy, and at a higher price, and you end up paying for them whether you want or not.

- Entitlements to groups that support the regime and the government, because entitlements are used to lock in political power.

- Every part of your life cycle is taken care of by the government and you have to submit to their policies.

- You personal freedoms are limited if they interfere with the interests of the government, freedoms are limited to areas where the government has no interest and you will be stunned how far government interest stretches.

- Excessive, intrusive, and bureaucratic tax control as the net tax paying minority realize that they will not even get close to get their money's worth of taxes delivered to the government and slowly start to try to avoid taxes as a natural reaction.

- Extensive interpretations of tax laws to avoid loop holes, and in a society where it all falls together with big government the legal rigor to uphold the citizens' rights diminish in the eyes of administrative courts as their role is less independent and glides down the slippery slope to solely serve the government's interest.

- As governmental dependency grows, people who are dependent on the government start to act as mind guards and create a pro-government group thinking to "protect" the society from any pro-liberty movements or reactions of fundamental critique of the way the society is structured.

Step by step our liberties are reduced and government takes a larger portion of our lives. The nationalization of the health care industry is absolutely necessary for the creation of a socialist society as it dramatically increases the population's dependency on the government and the removal of any individual self-reliance.

Socialized health care relies heavily on an ideological platform that is totally foreign to the American mind, history, and the American spirit.

It is socialism.

As the Swedish *Folkhemmet* was based on the notion that you are unable to organize your life and that it is instead the state that should organize it for you.

The Obamacare concept is tailored around the same principles of a socialist ideology. It might be presented in different ways but the bottom line is it has the same tenets.

The ideological platform that drives the debate for universal health care has a major assumption – you are unable to take care of your own business and the market is unable to cater to your needs, therefore, the market has to be wiped out and your money taken away so the government can fix it for you.

The Swedish socialist futuristic society, where the thought is that everything should be arranged for you from the cradle to the grave, started to crumble in the 1980s and has been slowly dismantled through the last two decades. Why does a governmental system not succeed over the market economy – but instead fails?

The decisions are made by bureaucrats who plan resources in a grand Soviet-style way with no ear to the rail and no ability to capture the needs of the population. There is no accountability of any significance, and the wellbeing of the patients is secondary to the interest of the government.

The Swedish politicians have learned the lesson – they have steadily returned to a market based solution because the citizens refused to pay a high price for second tier health care and started to demand value for their money or lower taxes.

One day even the citizens of the archetype nanny state said enough is enough.

It has been a slow but steady process. The government run health care has been forced to accept the reality that private actors are more effectively and efficiently able to provide health services. One of the major reasons for the Swedes to start privatizing health care is the fact that the waiting list for surgery and costs started to spin out of control.

It was a crumbling system that would collapse unless they started to create space for private enterprises to deliver health care services. The

Swedes had to adjust to the fact that it was an inferior system. The universal health care system is supplemented by private insurers who offer private health care when the public health care fails.

So when American activists, politicians, and lobbyists use Sweden and other European states as example of successful universal health care, many of their references are outdated and obsolete. It has already failed in Europe and been replaced with market driven solutions.

MAMMOTH ENTITIES

Socialized health care will slowly prevail over the private option, not by merit but by the fact that the ushers of the idea will legislate. This will start to reshape the political field. In Sweden, one of the largest proponents for leftist policies is the socialized health industry.

This entity operates as a substantial part of the economy that gives them a significant impact on local and state politics. In American terms, it means that the country will glide into pseudo-totalitarianism as swing states swung for the last time and become permanently voting Democrat. In many states it only takes a little, permanent political change to go from swing states to become solid Democratic states.

That would limit any other party to be able to compete. Universal health care is not a bipartisan construct. The health care public entity, which would be in many cases the largest employer in every town, county, and state, will have a political agenda distributed by its management that is politically hand-picked.

Suddenly 6 - 8% of the work force is no longer private employees, but public employees whom will realize that their wages are dependent on overspending politicians.

There are 14,000,000 employees in the health care sector, many of them working in hospitals and other larger institutions that, in a public system, will be under direct political influence and heavily unionized. By its sheer voting power, this would directly influence American politics in favor of big government. More than 70% of all hospital jobs are in establishments with over 1,000 workers. The health care industry will replace then unions as the backbone of the liberal machinery.

Once these mammoth entities, either full blown governmental health care institutions or public non for profits, start to operate, their influence will come naturally as their absolute size would generate political impact on the states they operate within.

Any fiscally balanced budget becomes politically impossible to pass. In many states only a fraction of that shift creates political hegemony. When these mammoth public health care providers are set up they will expand their realm based on health issues, either real or fabricated for political purposes, and intrude into other fields of our lives. And by doing so, play a role in defining society. We can not tell what organizational form an American national health care would have, but we know that a chain of entities that controls 16% of the economy will have an enormous impact on the political climate – as these entities will be heavily polarized towards the Democrats.

In Sweden, business leaders and small business owners avoid having a political view – or expressing opinions that would be in direct conflict with the leftist agenda as they heavily rely on business from the public sector. In many towns and counties the health care system is the largest employer and one of the largest purchasers of local professional services and products. Naturally, it leads to silencing any conservative and anti-socialist opinions in the local business communities.

If America decides to nationalize health care, this will have a direct impact on politics at every level as many outspoken Republican supporters will suddenly have to make a choice between supporting the Republican Party or protecting their business and livelihood. This is a far more dramatic change of financial support for a single party than Sweden.

Sweden has public funds given in any major election based on last election results. In America, especially in local politics, the fundraising is totally crucial for the success of the campaign and maintaining a healthy democracy. If that is taken out of play, then we are gliding into a form of soft dictatorship.

The pressure can easily increase to detach electoral support groups, such as churches and congregations, from the Republicans. The health care system can outsource and contract the independent health and senior care to faith based organizations but these contracts would be dependent on political loyalty. In reality, a church that supports the Republican stance in abortion and family values might have to drop that support to secure that they can maintain their senior home. The political black mail from the nationalized health care systems would be rampant.

If there are no private health care providers – but only one way to get health care, there will also only be one buyer of services like senior homes, rehab centers, medical professional service, and the whole procurement needed to operate hospitals, health clinics, and emergency facilities. When you are the only buyer on a market, you have the power to tell the market, if it is a market any longer or just a plain command chain, what you require and the sellers must comply if they want to stay in business.

The Republicans are by default under funded in a majority of the electoral districts in this country – this would change the game in a dramatic level as the Republicans are going to be so financially behind the Democrats that elections no longer will be fair. There will be a significant disadvantage for any Republican running for office as they will be unable to buy adequate advertisement, marketing, and get their message across to the voters en masse.

The nationalized health care entities will be fully unionized and the unions will support only one party – the Democrats. It is logical as only the Democrats would ensure that the nationalized health care is not questioned, stays unionized, and thoroughly politically managed and biased.

The majority of those who will be active as board members for these new public or semi-public health care entities are already activists or professional politicians. These entities become another political career path as they are government run, and they all share the same agenda. Big government is good and the bigger the better.

Any fiscally conservative outlook would be in direct conflict with the organization itself. So, even if admitted to any steering committee or board, those who favor fiscal conservatism and small government would have no voice in the organization since it is the juggernaut of big government.

GOVERNMENT BECOMES YOUR KID'S PARENT

In a universal health care system that eventually covers every individual that has a social security number, it will open the flood gates for minors making their own medical decisions without their parents' knowledge or consent. In the Swedish framework of government, government run youth clinics are tied to schools so underage minors have access to nurses and even doctors on their own. The underage youth can get prescription medicine and medical advice without notification or parental consent. Any form of birth control is administered to minors that are below the legal age to engage in sex.

For the government, morality is not an issue but the cost of underage motherhood is. This creates an environment where government sets the stage for an early loss of virginity once it ensured that there would be no costly expenses for the government. The outlook is utilitarian and driven by leftist policies that promote sexual liberties. In reality it creates a social problem where older teenage boys prey upon younger girls. The boys know that the younger girls can easily obtain prescription birth control without parental consent.

The parent loses the control over their child's health care decision as the system will deliver services to them as soon as they are considered sexually able to engage in intercourse. That does not take in to consideration their physical, psychological, and emotional maturity. The liberal tenets of the society have, over time, marginalized the power of the parent and replaced it with the government.

It might sound free spirited and open minded to enable youth to engage in relationships without having the risk of pregnancy – seen from an American liberal outlook but it also comes with an emotional price as youth are catapulted into adulthood when the sexually active age is as low as 12 or 13 years of age. The natural emotional maturity that grows over time is trespassed and it has a price.

The counterargument is naturally that all these procedures are a way to prevent teenage pregnancies. That could be done without putting 13 year old girls on "the pill" as condoms can be bought at any pharmacy or supermarket.

The school clinics would also treat sexually transmitted deceases without parental knowledge. In real terms the children are left alone in a world that they hardly understand and the government takes over the role as informer, parent, and provider. The government takes no responsibility for the emotional damages to children who are thrown into adulthood and the sexual behaviors of adults. The government only watches over its own interest.

This total disrespect for parental rights is synonymous with the public health care system's treatment of other rights as privacy and patient's rights.

ABORTION AS BIRTH CONTROL

As the debate about public health care has developed, one of the key questions has been abortion. All the countries that have universal single payer health care systems have abortion as a part of the health care coverage provided by the public health care system and it is paid for by public funds. All these countries have a far more non-restrictive approach to abortion and it is easily available for those women who seek the procedure.

The state has no interest in paying the social costs for young mothers or children born out of wedlock. Health care professionals will carry out this utilitarian duty by indirectly pushing for abortion.

The procedure is readily available for every mother that wants it with full anonymity from her own family. The universal health care system in Sweden utilizes privacy legislation to prevent parents from knowing what happens with their children. The administrative legal system considers it harms the child if the parents are informed about their child's abortion procedure. The child can make any decision on their own from an early age and the universal health care is there to provide it as long as it goes along the policy and guidelines of the system itself.

In Sweden, abortions have been performed on girls as young as 11-year old without informing their parents about the pregnancy or the abortion. The ability to get birth control at an early age lowers the actual age when teens start to engage in sexual activity. So these minors who end up pregnant at an early age are a product of a changing social pattern that comes with the governmental interference in the parents' upbringing of the child, transfer of moral values, and control. The easy access to abortion gives it the role of a back up birth control as the minors who engage in sex know that they would have access to abortion without any interference from their parents.

When the universal health care system and its counselors advise the child, it assumes that the child could make the decision that is best for her. In reality, the counselors and social workers would, intended or unintended, put the child under pressure to perform an abortion if they are minors. My critique is mainly that the parents are taken out from the decision process and they are the defendants of the child's interest. They have custody and it is their child.

Even if they come to the same conclusion as the social workers, they are still parents and a supporter for the child. Instead, a scared teenager makes all these decisions in a clinical environment.

It is horrifying that a child has to make life and death decisions about their child surrounded by publicly employed social workers or health care counselors. Naturally, the child can voluntarily speak with their parents but the privacy protection within the public health care abortion option is inviting as they do not have to face their parents with reality and it is a quick fix for the moment. A pre-teenager or teenager does not have the emotional maturity to fully understand the consequences and the impact over time.

The state doesn't want childbearing teens - it disrupts schooling and increases pressure on social services, and the dehumanized practice continues, as this is solely governmental business. Your child's unborn offspring is now governmental property. We have to remember what will steer these public health care entities – nominees that are preferred by the proponents of the system and these board members will be pro-abortion activists, political nominees, loyalists to the leftist agenda, and liberal career politicians. There will be no pro-life voice heard once this is a reality.

This especially blatant idea is the "Plan B" discussion as these entities will not be governmental entities but instead private non for profits with tremendous backing of taxpayers money easily given out by the liberal and leftist politicians that rule Congress today. These private entities would get the governmental money but there is no transparency, real accountability, or taxpayer's control of what is really happening with their money.

So, the notion that there will not be any funding of abortions with taxpayer's dollars is easily nullified and is a bone thrown to the opposition to silence them; however, in the long run, the socialized health care would be the biggest proponents of pro-abortion in the country and they will carry out more abortions than any other entity.

We used to say that we get what we pay for and it is true when it comes to socialized medicine – not what you pay for it through taxes but the political message that the leftist can get through by actually being those who use your taxpayer money to fund these entities. The socialized health care is an activist driven idea and these activists are highly pro-abortion. They will form the boards, the committees, the steering group, the policy makers, and set the agenda for these entities. That makes the analogy with Sweden very functional, step by step, and retreats as the concept of "Plan B" is just another way to move it forward by not a straight out take over by socialized health care but by incremental steps that lead to big changes over time.

These entities would also receive funding from other sources. Even funding at the state level would have a political signal woven into the transaction – it is assumed that a pro-abortion stance is taken.

Sweden introduced abortion legislation in 1938 but the current abortion legislation is from 1975 and allows free abortion. The number of surgical abortions in Sweden is not significantly higher than the United States. The difference is that Sweden offers different non-surgical solutions for early termination that will not appear in a statistical comparison.

SUING THE HEALTH CARE SYSTEM? FORGET IT!

The Swedish health care system is set up to handle complaints by funneling them to a Patient Injury Board. Even if there is gross malpractice, still the compensation is marginal, the required level of proof is high, and it is largely a pointless exercise.

America might be overly litigious but this is at the other end of the pendulum - you can't practically sue the health care provider in Sweden. You as an individual have very limited rights against the public health care mammoth. Why? The government has no interest letting people who lost a leg, a family member, or been disabled for life by doctors' malpractice to walk away with millions in compensation. The government has better plans for the money, according to themselves, than paying for the damages, the pain, and the suffering of those who get hurt and harmed in the health care system.

If you combine legislative government, the health care system, and the courts to the same overhead, patient's rights are gone. With the fully developed universal health care system, you have to accept the treatment you are given. Even if the treatment is disastrous - you have to live with it.

The ability to sue for negligence and malpractice is a corner stone of patient's rights. Without these rights, you will be at the mercy of the public health care system. When no one is held accountable for their mistakes, naturally the number of mistakes increases as there are no safeguards in taking risks with your health and life. It does not need to be intentional – it becomes a system that does not punish gross malpractice or negligence and with that comes a higher degree of risk taking behavior with other humans' health and life.

In the 1970s in Sweden, my dad was healthy and a hard working editor-in-chief for a regional newspaper. He developed a headache that did not want to leave him. He went to a doctor that ordered a contrast x-ray, which he had performed at the Uppsala Hospital. It went terribly wrong and my father never recovered from the damages.

A small part of tissue was scraped from one of the veins when they entered the needle and migrated to the brain creating a blockage that put him in critical condition and almost killed him on the spot. Afterwards, we were informed that the actual staging with the contrast fluid and needle was made by medical students under the supervision of a licensed doctor. They made a mistake. My dad's thirty year professional career was lost in a fraction of seconds. His physical ability to write with a typewriter and parts of his mobility were lost, and he was catapulted into years of rehabilitation with no real improvements in his condition.

He died a few years later as a result of a damaged heart. The heart had been severely damaged as part of the physical shock during the hospital accident. He was predestined from the day when the students made their mistake to die within a couple of years and he knew it.

The case went to Patient Injury Board. Although my parents were well educated and experienced to fight it to the bitter end, the system prevailed. The system will consistently prevail in any nationalized health care system. If you have the legislator, the courts, and the health care system as parts of the government, these "players" will ensure the interest of the government and no one else.

My dad's retirement compensation was that he was given an early retirement with compensation equal to 90% of his salary that he had earned at the newspaper until he became 65 years old and entered the official retirement age. He died at 60 years old, so they even saved on that.

The financial compensation was $3,000 to fund for specialized tools for disabled, a typewriter for disabled, and other rehab utilities. That was it.

The hospital and health care system almost kills a person by an obvious mistake by medical students that are given the chance to do "the real stuff" without the patient even knowing it – and they fail. It results in that the patient loses a long and distinguished career as a newspaper man, his finer motion, becomes unable to typewrite or even write easily read handwritten notes – and eventually kills him twenty years earlier than a normal life lasts. The total financial compensation: retirement and $3,000 in disability tools.

A socialized health care system that is directly linked to any public expenditure for its upholding will, by its construct, be driven to block patients' rights as these rights increase the cost.

The easiest way is to create, like in Sweden, different levels of complaint organizations, but prevent any legal action and, by doing so, defuse the patient's right to compensation for gross negligence and malpractice. If government is your health care provider, you will have very limited possibilities to get the compensation you deserve. The beauty for the government is that they control the legislature, the health care system, and they are paying, so why should the government "give away" money if they can keep it and do other things with it within the law?

The closer you get to the self-interest of the government, the odder the interpretation of the law. If the government has a well-defined self-interest to preserve resources and keep costs low in a socialized health care system, the actors will follow, as the actors are public entities and employees, which will limit the patient's ability to get their rights. The government has absolutely no incentive to protect patient rights and secure that those are upheld through the health care system.

SOVIET-STYLED REDISTRIBUTION

Every Swede pays an average of 13% of their salary no matter their income or health care needs to the health care system. So, if you earn $60,000 you pay $7,800, but if you and your spouse make both $60,000, the total price you pay as a couple $15,600 for health care. Already at yearly incomes of $25,000 you start to pay more than you statistically would need. Let's say that you hit it big and suddenly made $300,000 every year. You, and that is only you not your family, will pay $39,000 for your personal health care. Universal single payer health care system will be more expensive once in place for the average working family. For free riders and illegal immigrants, this is heaven.

It is obvious that single payer universal health care in the United States without slashing Medicare would need as in Sweden 13% or more of the income of those who are working. If your tax is today 40% and 13% are added your new tax would be 53%. It is a 30% increase. To raise taxes by 30% is unprecedented. Even if the system will not be based on wage tax but instead a fee, it is likely that poverty mitigating programs would pick up the final bill and illegal immigrants get their fee waived, as they do not earn money on payroll.

The federal government has a history, or, put it this way, the Congress has a history of creating federal programs that waives fees and costs under a specific poverty level so we can assume with confidence that it will happen in a universal health care system. On paper, everyone will pay but in reality maybe 1 out of 3 will have a fee waiver, federal or state reimbursement, or any other program that removes their cost and transfers it to the other 2 out of 3.

We have not even discussed the fact that over 65 million American do not pay taxes at all and you can easily add to that 12 million illegal aliens that work and live in the "off the books" economy who will not contribute to the universal health care system.

Someone has to pay, especially since the federal government, after a tsunami of fiscal irresponsibility, has opened the floodgates for long running and severe deficits. There is no way that the federal government can pick up the bill for budget deficits in a nationalized health care system. These adjustments will have to be made in other ways than through federal funds. It can only be addressed in three ways – lower the level of delivered service, raise taxes, or extended waiting lists. The waiting lists could be seen as a lower level of service but I wanted to visualize that they can cut in both ends – you have to wait longer for less.

Any demographic change in society will eventually increase the stress of the nationalized health care system like longevity, the acceptance of illegal immigrants into the system, unhealthy work habits, and socioeconomic changes and raised taxes. You might feel that you have nothing to do with it – but with a nationalized health care system the problems of others would directly impact your wallet.

The Swedish share of GDP that is consumed by health care is circa 9 – 10% meanwhile the American health care industry has a 16% share of the GDP. The leftist argument is that the Swedish system covers everyone and that it is cheaper.

The problem is that no one compares services rendered, when they are provided, and other factors as system differences. If the American system had the tenets of the Swedish system – as inability for patients to sue the health care system, then the cost for the American system would go down dramatically as a major part of the additional tests that are taken in order to ensure that good practice is followed and avoid any liability. If there is no liability whatsoever you can create dramatic savings in health care, but the service rendered would be completely different to the quality we are used to at American hospitals.

The Swedish system is fully based on redistribution – not only of money but also services. In a universal health care system everyone is provided the same service in theory.

In reality, the redistribution will have side effects like any socialist system with widespread favoritism, wheeling and dealing, reliance of connections and other forms of corruption.

POPULATION REGISTRY AND CONTROL

In a nationalized health care system, you need to know who is who – otherwise the system could never be able determine who is entitled. The structure depends on how the system is created and designed, but with a nationalized health care system you will be tracked by the state where you reside and how you move in a manner that is unseen in America. The nationalized health care system becomes a vehicle for population control.

If you leave the United States and are no longer a resident of the state, even if you are a citizen and might maintain a driving license, you will have to report immediately if you want to avoid the 13% health care tax. I use the number 13% as it is in Sweden to exemplify the actual tax pressure that is laid upon you for the nationalized health care.

Let's say you moved and you do not want to pay the 13% tax for services you do not receive, can receive, or want to taken out from the tax roll. The mammoth entity has no interest to let you go so easy. You will end up having to reveal your private life –

partner, dwellings, travel, money, and job to prove your case that you have the right to leave the public health care system and do not need to pay the tax. If you have to seek an appeal, your information could be a part of administrative court documents that are open and public documents. As soon as you return to the United States, you will be automatically enrolled again and the taxes start to pile up.

Public universal health care has no interest in protecting your privacy. They want their tax money and, to fight for your rights, you will have to prove that you meet the requirements to not be taxable. In that process, your private life is up for display.

The national ID-card and national population registry that includes your medical information is a foundation of the nationalized health care system. You can see where this is going – population control and ability to use the law and health care access to map your whole private life in public searchable databases owned and operated by the government.

By operating an impeccable population registry that tracks where you live, who you live with, when you move and your citizen status including residency the Swedes can separate who can receive universal health care from those not entitled. The Swedish authorities will know if you have a Swedish social security number, with the tap of the keyboard, more information about yourself than you can remember. The Swedish government has taken sharing of information between agencies to a new level. The reason is very simple – to collect health care tax and suppress any tax evasion.

It is heavily centralized and only the central administration can change the registered information in the data. So if you want to change your name, even the slightest change, you have to file an application at a national agency that processes your paperwork. This centralized population registry makes it possible to determine who is who under all circumstances and it is necessary for the national health care system. Otherwise, any person could claim to be entitled.

To implement that in the United States requires a completely new doctrine for population registry and control. In an American context that would require that every existing driving license had to be voided and reapplied under stricter identification rules that would match not only data from Internal Revenue Service, state government, municipal government, Social Security Administration, and Department of Homeland Security but almost any agency that provides services to the general public. The reason why a new population registry would be needed in the United States is the fact that lax rules dating back to the 1940s up until the War on Terrorism, and stricter identification criteria following 9/11, has made a significant percentage of personal information about individuals questionable.

If America instead neglects maintaining secure records, determining eligibility for public health care would not be possible and the floodgates for fraud would open and rampant misuse of the system would prevail. This would eventually bring down the system.

It is financially impossible to create a universal health care system without clearly knowing who is entitled and not. The system needs to have limits of its entitlement. A social security number would not be enough as these numbers have been handed out through decades to temporary residents that might not even live in the United States or might today be out of status as illegal immigrants.

The Congress has investigated the cost of many of the "public options", but still we have no clear picture of the actual realm of the group that would be entitled and under which conditions. The risk is political. It is very easy for political reasons to extend the entitlement. Politicians would have a hard time being firm on illegal immigrants' entitlement, as that would put the politicians on a collision course with mainly the Hispanic community as they represent a significant part of the illegal immigrants. So the easy sell is then that everyone that is a legal resident alien or citizen can join according to one fee plan and then the illegal immigrants can join according to a different fee structure. That assumes that they actually pay the fee which is a wild guess as they are likely to be able to get access to service without having to state that they are illegal immigrants.

It would work politically – but again – without an impeccable population registry and control over who is who on a national level, this is unlikely to succeed. The system would be predestined to fail because of lack of funds. If you design a system to provide the health care needs for a population and then increase that population without any additional funds – then naturally it would lead to a lower level of service, declined quality, and waiting lists for complex procedures. In real terms, American health care goes from being a first world system to a third world system.

Thousands, if not a million, American residents live as any other American citizen but they are still not in good standing with their immigration even if they have been here for ten or fifteen years. A universal health care system will raise issues about who is entitled and who is not.

The alternative is for an American universal health care system to surrender to the fact that there is no order in the population registry and just provide health care for everyone who shows up. If that is done, costs will dramatically increase at some level depending on who will pick up the bill – the state government, the federal government, or the public health care system.

Illegal immigrants that have arrived within the last years and make up a significant population would create an enormous pressure on a universal health care, if implemented, in states like Texas and California. If they are given universal health care, it would be a pure loss for the system as they mostly work for cash. They will never be payees into the universal health care system as it is based on salary taxes, and they do not file taxes.

The difference is that Sweden has almost no illegal immigrants compared to the United States. The Swedes do not provide health care services for illegal immigrants and the illegal immigrants can be arrested and deported if they require public service without good legal standing.

This firm and uniform standpoint towards illegal immigration is necessary to avoid a universal health care system from crumbling down and to maintain a sustainable ratio between those who pay into the system and those who benefit from it.

The working middle class that would be the backbone to pay into the system would not only face that their existing health care is halved in its service value – but most likely face higher cost of health care as they will be the ones to pick up the bill.

The universal health care system would have maybe 60 million to 70 million "free riders" if based on wage taxes, and maybe half if based on fees, that will not pay anything into the system. We already know that approximately 60 million Americans pay no taxes as adults add to that the estimated 10-15 million illegal immigrants.

There is no way that a universal health care system can be viably implemented unless America creates a population registry that can identify the entitlements for each individual and that would have to be designed from scratch to a high degree as we can not rely on driver's license data as the quality would be too low – too many errors.

Many illegal immigrants have both social security numbers and driver's licenses as these were issued without rigorous control of status before 9/11. The alternative is that you had to show a US passport or a valid foreign passport with a green card to be able to register.

Another problematic task is the number of points of registration. If the registration is done by hospitals – and not a federal agency – then it is highly likely that registration fraud would be rampant. It would be very easy to trespass the control of eligibility if it is registered and determined by a hospital clerk. This supports that the eligibility has to be determined by a central administration that has a vast access to data and information about our lives, income, and medical history. If one single registration at a health care provider or hospital would guarantee you free health care for life and there is no rigorous and audited process – then it is a given that corruption, bribery, and fraud would be synonymous with the system.

This requires a significant level of political strength to confront and set the limits for who is entitled – and here comes the real problem – selling out health care to get the votes of the free riders. It is apparent that the political power of the "free" health care promise is extremely high.

A promise that can not alienate anyone as a tighter population registry would upset the Hispanic population, as many of the illegal immigrants are Hispanics – and many Hispanics might be citizens by birth but their elderly parents are not. Would the voting power of the younger Hispanics act to put pressure to extend health care to elderly that are not citizens? Yes, naturally, as every group tries to maximize its own self-interest.

The risk is, even with an enhanced population registry, that the group of entitled would expand and put additional burden on the system beyond what it was designed for. That could come though political wheeling and dealing, sheer inability from an administrative standpoint to identify groups, or systematic fraud within the system itself.

We can speculate about the outcome but the challenges are clear. This also represents a new threat to the privacy and respect for the private sphere of the citizenry as an increased population registration and control empowers the government with more accurate information about our lives and the way we live our lives. Historically, has any government when given the opportunity to get power taken that opportunity and given that power back to the people after the initial objective was reached? Governments like to stick to power.

To ensure the universal health care system is designed to function as intended it, would require procedures that would limit fraud, amass a significant amount of personal information, have access to all your medical data, and also determine who you are beyond any doubt. Just to be able to determine if you are entitled or not and, track the expenditures you generate.

The aggregation of these data could also open the floodgates for any data mining within these data under the pure excuse that it would help the universal health care system to better "serve you" and lower the costs.

To lower the costs also means to identify which procedures should not be done on which type of patients as it is not viable based on the government's interest to optimize your productivity under your life cycle. The collection of data has a tendency to look inviting and good when we start to collect it but aggregated data and personal information creates a deep intrusion in our privacy.

TAXES, TAXES, TAXES – AND MORE TAX MEN

The nationalized health care system would rely on taxes and that requires that the tax base increases – and it means that government will have to tax more, control harder, inspect more, and suppress "off the books" labor. You can not put the whole burden of the nationalized health care on the population that have full tax exposure and let others free ride. Even the Europeans know that the system would break down by kicking the W2 and 1099 tax brackets far above 50 – 60% at its highest level.

If you compare American tax control with the tax authorities in Europe, and especially Sweden, the American Internal Revenue Service is less intrusive, aggressive, and require less financial documentation as their European counterparts.

To be able to pay for the nationalized health care, the Internal Revenue Service and all other tax efforts have to be not only increased but maybe doubled as they have to ensure that everyone that should pay actually is paying. A nationalized health care system would create a need to audit more people, have a significantly higher number of tax agents out on the streets looking for any "off the books" business, and stricter laws about small businesses and their accounting.

There is no way that you can implement a nationalized health care system as long as you have to accept that maybe 10% of the economy is "off the books." When you look on the cash market, it actually represents a higher degree of the tax base for nationalized health care than it represents of the economy because its funding is derived from wage taxes.

The difference is that Sweden has almost no illegal immigrants compared to the United States. The Swedes does not provide health care services for illegal immigrants and the illegal immigrants can be arrested and deported if they require public service without good legal standing. So America is worse off trying to collect the taxes to pay for a universal health care system. Too many American residents do not pay taxes.

The cash economy becomes more attractive as taxes increase and if we add in Sweden's 13% additional taxes that nationalized health care will add, increasing the tax bracket to 40% to 53%, then naturally tax evasion will be rampant. Government will be forced to ensure that you and everybody else are paying their dues. You might not have contemplated evading taxes but the European experience shows that once taxes starts to climb over 45 – 50% the majority of the citizens are open to take risks with tax evasion. As soon as a tax bracket gets closer to 50% a natural law takes over and citizens start to wonder why they are having a hard time paying their bills, providing for their family, and why they primarily should be a producer of government revenues.

The question is relevant – but the government has no interest in the answer as it clashes with their self-interest. So, what have the Europeans done to be able to increase and maintain a tax base to pay for their nationalized health care? They have a tax law enforcement that is unheard of in America. The Swedes have taken it as far as you are guilty for tax evasion until – you can prove that you are innocent (!). A judicial thought that is completely opposite to the tradition in the Western world were you are innocent until proven guilty – but governments can go far to squeeze out their taxes.

You might not even believe it yet so I have to write it twice – the Swedish tax authority and tax laws assumes that you are evading taxes, if questioned by authorities, until you can prove that you are innocent.

The burden of proof is on the defendant, not the accuser. To any freedom loving and liberty defending American this sounds like tyranny and it is not far fetched. Any government that can accuse its citizens for illegal activities and flip the burden of proving the innocence, or guilt, to the defendants have stepped out of the boundaries of any rule of law that respects human rights.

Does it matter? No – because if they do not do it then tax evasion would be undermining the leftist hegemony and the so called "welfare state" and its main foundation – the nationalized health care system. In the same way as the Soviet Union had to put dissidents in mental institutions to quiet them – the "welfare state" has to use extreme tax laws to squeeze out the money from their citizens to fund a redistribution from which they do not benefit.

Redistribution is a nicer way to say that you take money from the hard working people to reward those who you want to be rewarded. In return they become politically loyal to you and work as vehicles for political dominance. Increased tax control also needs to create check points in society that would pick up any cash transactions to force the cash to be visible – and expose the cash economy to the tax authorities and their inquiries.

In Sweden if you deposit $3,500 or more in cash into a banking account, by law you have to explain how you legally obtained the money.

The push to force people to feel like criminals and always be ready to explain how they can have money serves three purposes – it cracks down on the cash economy, it forces transactions from the cash economy into the "white economy", and last but not least, it is a power game when the citizens never can feel that their prosperity and equity is truly theirs. The repeated questioning from the government pursuing to soak up as much money as possible in taxes has a hidden but obvious message – your wealth is temporarily yours, but in the long run it belongs to the government.

Today 65 - 70 million American do not pay taxes. If America picks a universal health care system based on wage taxes or fees tied to wages, the government must address the fact that a significant number of Americans will not pay into the system. The alternative is to create a system that would draw its money from corporate taxes and capital gains, which would be a recipe for disaster as America already has, by international standards, high taxes on corporations and capital gains. That would be a disastrous move that would increase the flight of capital and jobs from America instead of supporting a healthy recovery of the economy.

Somebody has to pay. If we want to serve as many as possible, they have to pay as well. Otherwise the system will be unbalanced and lead to a collapse. It can take different turns by either increased tax evasion, the system no longer serves it purpose, or a political rebellion from the middle class that actually carries the tax burden of this country.

DECLINE IN PROFESSIONALISM

If you compare the universal health care systems that exist in the world, you see that they have two main things in common – it is based on taxes with no correlation between what you pay into the system and what you get and that the medical staff when compared to American staff are hired at far lower compensation levels.

A registered nurse in Sweden makes about $3,000 a month before tax with very limited extra compensation for specialization. American nurses earn at least 40 - 50% more. If an American nurse gets a specialization in a sought after field, the American can earn double compared to the Swedish nurse.

A doctor earns in Sweden about $50,000 - $70,000 on average, which is about half or less than the salary a doctor in America can expect. Another factor that makes the difference even bigger is the additional upside that allows American doctors through private practice and specialization to reach income levels that are far higher than the average doctor. These options are limited in Sweden.

It does not directly follow that health care workers and doctors in Sweden are less competent, but salary actually matters when it comes to career decisions. The best and the brightest in the United States see health care as a career path. It is important for you as a patient that health care is attractive as a career because that would give you more competent care givers as the competition to have these jobs increases.

If health care is seen as a less viable route, those who pick that track either do it from an inner calling and personal interest or it becomes an option for those with less options to choose from.

That will result in a decline in professionalism that gives the health care industry, and its participants, less of a political and public voice as the status of the industry is lower in the eyes of the public. Maybe that does not reflect their actual abilities, but status is perception and perception drives people's thoughts.

If you are sick, have a critical injury, or suffer from a life threatening disease, you want the best and the brightest to be your doctors. In a universal socialized health care system that might not be the case because other careers will pay far more for those who are gifted and are able to grasp complex problems and deliver solutions. That could be a life and death decision. Health care decisions are made through our entire life span and mistakes add up.

The universal health care system has an emphasis on providing care on a reactive basis instead of preventive care, which often prevents illnesses or detects their presence at an early stage. That leads to slower detection of any health care issue; adds to the actual existence of waiting lists due to the universal health care system's high burden of promises to deliver in relation to their actual resources, and then you staff the system with nurses and doctors that earn slightly more than the guy that drives the Greyhound bus or a plumber. They might even earn less than the plumber.

The plumber can make mistakes at work and there will be a leak or a flooding but in most cases that is marginal and can be fixed without permanent damage.

If a doctor or nurse makes a mistake at work it can be lethal, and if not deadly, there is a high risk that the damages will be permanent and lead to pain and injury for the affected patient.

Let us now combine two of the tenets of the universal health care system – underpaid nurses and doctors together with the fact that patients' rights are marginalized and it is almost impossible to sue the health care system. If the staff is underpaid, the hiring process will be forced to be more lenient to applicants that might not be as qualified because there is not an adequate pool of highly qualified and interested applicants – the risk of incompetence is there.

Any work place that has a hard time providing a market level salary will have incompetence by some of their employees as they have to extend the circle of applicants beyond the ideal candidates, and, in a universal health care system, they are protected because it is impossible to sue the health care system.

The way the system in designed and the lack of accountability creates risks that are not mitigated in any way and the risk is transferred to the patient, without their knowledge and consent, and, if there is an incident, the patient ends up paying the full price with no compensation from the socialized health care system.

It might look like a major cost saving to start paying nurses and doctors' lower salaries but the actual cost in human suffering is not taken into account. One of the liberal and leftist arguments for the universal health care system is lower costs but when you take a deep look into these so called "deeper looks," you will see that it is not a matter of waste but instead a question about services rendered and by whom.

In the health care debate many of the liberal proponents of socialized medicine make comparisons between two completely different systems. The Swedish health care system costs about 10% of GDP and the American system needs 50% more. At first glance the argument for savings in a universal health care system makes sense as there actually is such a large difference in resources dedicated to health care. This argument would be valid if we were comparing apples to apples, but we are not.

If the American health care salaries were cut in half that would make it cheaper, as the Swedish salaries are only half of the Americans. Salaries are one of the largest costs for health care providers. If it was impossible to sue your health care provider it would also be cheaper. Add to that the limited, if any, preventive care that is given in socialized medicine and you will see that the differences in actual costs are marginal. Socialized medicine is not the cost-effective and efficient alternative – they just pay less, give less, and take less responsibility.

It is essential that medical treatments are decided by doctors – and not politicians. One of the tenets of the American health care system is the high degree of professional freedom for doctors to choose which approach to take to different medical problems and also, in an early stage, prescribe targeted, aggressive treatments. In the current American health care system, emphasis is placed upon preventive care such as annual physicals and screenings based on your family history. In a universal health care system, the resource base is not adequate to continue this level of preventive care.

That professional freedom is not measurable or something we are able to quantify into statistical numbers, but it is a cornerstone for a high level of quality and professionalism. In socialized medicine those decisions are made by politically appointed boards and committees based on the feasibility seen from the system itself and not the individual's need for care.

STEPPINGSTONE TO ANOTHER SOCIETY

The universal health care system, which will start small and with the support of its ushers claim a larger and larger territory, is a vital vehicle for those who want to transform the free people of America to a collective herd of subjects for the government.

It might start as a non for profit organization that can not make it financially and then get taken over by the government – as the so called "Plan B" tries to camouflage public health care as a freestanding non for profit organization. For those who propose "Plan B", "Plan C", and "Plan D" it is a tactical move in politics when they are really aiming for "Plan A". We do not hear so much about "Plan A", but "Plan A" is the single payer universal health care system as I have described it. The huge public health care system that is more political than medical.

Proponents of universal health care sees you as a resource for the government and the focus has completely shifted from being about you, as citizen and a part of the public, to the interest of the government.

It might sound far fetched but when people are a cost and a burden the fastest way for the government to cut costs is to let them go – not directly by involuntary euthanasia but by restricting care to groups that are considered less valuable seen from the governmental interest.

A single payer universal health care system, and all experience speaks in that direction, is heavily underfunded leading to ongoing revisions of the policies for supplying care. If the public health care provider has to prioritize between a 25-year old, an infant, and an elderly person it will naturally prioritize the 25-year old as that individual represents an investment in schooling that is just waiting to payoff in productivity and tax revenues. The utilitarian view of the government is completely different from yours – or any other individual. The government wants to provide enough health care that keeps people content, tax them for that service, and avoid costly treatments to individuals that will never pay back into the system through taxes.

The elderly are no longer net payers to the government as they no longer work or pay taxes as they used to do. They are a pure cost with social security pay outs. If the elderly are given less care that would decrease their longevity by a few years, but the health care system will save money.

Swedish studies show that 7% of those on the waiting list for heart surgery would die before they have a chance to receive treatment. Naturally, 1 – 2% would die even in the best of systems, but the other 5% die because the system prefers them to die instead of improving services.

If they die, the cost is gone as they are gone – and the savings are huge as the government no longer has to pay for treatment, rehabilitation, hospitals, outpatient care, transportation, and the biggest cost saving – decades of social benefits and social security as many heart surgery patients are in their 60s.

No diabolic force would actively work to shorten the life of the elderly. It will just be the effect of the allocation of resources, and government will silently agree. If two million elderly, who get $20,000 a year from the social security and other support from the federal government live three year less, the total savings would be $120,000,000,000 or in other words – 40 billion dollars a year.

Now we run the numbers in the other direction. Let's say they instead live three years longer that means that suddenly the government has to find 40 billion dollars a year to pay for this extra longevity. We are just running the numbers here to show where it goes.

If the government suddenly ends up with elderly that keep living, they have no fiscal plan to deal with it. The deficit is already so deep that it would be a fiscal catastrophe. That is the problem when you have a single payer universal health care system. The health care provider benefits greatly if longevity shortens. As an elderly person, you are a "burden" in a budget context.

The counterargument would be that private insurance companies have no interest in financial terms of longevity, and it is true, but they have law suits, laws, federal, state, and local government that control that they conduct their business in an ethical way.

In a single payer universal health care system all those checks and balances, or call them control functions, are gone or are severely downsized. It's just the simple fact that your ability to file a successful lawsuit has been drastically reduced. It takes away your own, and your family's, option to start a investigation with the possibility of being awarded damages after you, or anyone in your family, have been the victim of gross negligence and malpractice.

The most vulnerable groups in this transition are the elderly and the unborn children, as they have little leverage in this new leftist hegemony that is totally driven from a rationale that is in direct contrast to traditional American family values.

The interest of the state and the government supersedes the interest of the individual. When there is a conflict of interest, the government always wins and that policy is institutionalized, public, and clear.

There is no utilitarian reason for the government to even care what you as an individual really need or think. The powers of the institutionalized leftist hegemony will defuse the impact of elections as they will provide resources and support to those who promote their cause.

These actions are seen as democratic and constitutional but in reality it gives us a society that resembles a dictatorship. Like any political hegemony that is based on vote buying, unless raw violence and force is used, national health care is one of the most effective machines for vote buying as it has a tremendous "redistributing" power.

Why is it a prime target for the left to drive it through Congress, even if it starts out camouflaged as "public option" or the Trojan horse "Plan B", if they do not seek to utilize its political power?

Any political group, as the left and represented in this present presidential administration, who considers that they know best what the citizens want – even better than the citizens themselves – will seek power and tools of power.

For leftist power means tools to change and form the society according to their beliefs, and they need system-sized power houses to drive change through the existing society as they firmly understand that the citizens will object to these changes.

Politics are about power and politicians have always tried to take a larger and larger territory in our lives as they try to maximize their sphere of influence. The sudden need to socialize health care is not as sudden as it seems; it is what many leftists have waited decades for and they now race to seize the opportunity.

In a recession, with increasing pressure on unemployed and social stress, the idea of universal health care gets fast traction in the public debate as it sounds like a solution that will solve many challenges, be cheaper, reduce waste, and maintain quality. That equation will never work.

It is a political pipe dream that has to come with a price, either in more money or loss of benefits, quality of services rendered, and fewer services provided compared to what people received earlier for the same cost.

Universal health care is not the right option for America to solve the existing problems within the health care system. Universal health care already has too many flaws and hurdles to be successfully implemented in America. Naturally, if you seek limitless political power and want to steer America towards socialism, then universal health care fits your agenda. Then it is wielded as a vehicle to power.

Universal health care is not about your health or your ability to get professional care; it is solely about political power.

This governmental health care system will not only determine life and death based on the economic outlook of the government, but also erase family values as it paves the way for a reshaped nation that no longer represents the ideals of freedom, liberty, and protection of individual rights that the founding fathers so wisely gave this country.

NOTES

These notes contain additional reading and for those texts that are in Swedish they can be translated by Google Translate. Copy the text into Google Translate and the result should be satisfying from Swedish to English. To make it easier to type in the URL a shorten URL is added from the web service Tinyurl. That is a link that leads to the original page but will save you time to type. The service can be found on the web at http://www.tinyurl.com.

Introduction

Democrats reach deal on health care, accessed 12/08/09
http://www.reuters.com/article/idUSTRE5B807720091209

http://tinyurl.com/health-care-deal

Only because it was impossible to push it through Congress does not remove the fact that the push for public health care will continue, accessed 1/16/10

http://articles.latimes.com/2009/dec/09/nation/la-na-health-senate9-2009dec09
http://tinyurl.com/hcdeal

"Gang of 10" pushes public option deal, accessed 12/08/09

http://firstread.msnbc.msn.com/archive/2009/12/08/2145561.aspx

http://tinyurl.com/pushpublic

Politically Managed Health Care – Do You Want It?

R.N Mats Sjöling, R.N. Ylva Ågren, Niclas Olofsson, R.N. Ove Hellzèn and R.N. Kenneth Asplund, *"Waiting for Surgery; Living a Life On Hold - A Continuous Struggle Against A Faceless System,"* International Journal of Nursing Studies, 2005, Vol. 42, p. 544.

Sven R. Larson. "Lessons from Sweden's Universal Health System: Tales from the Health-care Crypt." Journal of American Physicians and Surgeons. 2008. Vol. 13 Number 1, as accessed 2/7/10

http://www.jpands.org/vol13no1/larson.pdf

Plan B

The whole debate about "Plan B" and the different options are well-documented on the web so I advise you to Google for "plan B" and "health care".

The Swedish Concept

Sweden's Single-Payer Health System Provides a Warning to Other Nations, accessed 1/10/10

http://www.nationalcenter.org/NPA555_Sweden_Health_Care.html

http://tinyurl.com/swedishhealthcare

Platsbrist hotar säkerheten (Swedish), *accessed* 1/10/10

http://www.lakartidningen.se/07engine.php?articleId=12337

http://tinyurl.com/congestion1

Richard W. Rahn has written a well formulated article about Sweden, accessed 1/16/10

http://www.cato.org/pub_display.php?pub_id=10462

http://tinyurl.com/Rahn-Sweden3

The history behind the nationalization of Swedish pharmacies in 1970 (Swedish), accessed 1/16/10

http://www.lakemedelsvarlden.se/zino.aspx?articleID=727

http://tinyurl.com/pharma2

Henry J. Kaiser Family foundation has an informative site about American health care costs, accessed 1/18/10

http://www.kaiseredu.org/topics_im.asp?imID=1&parentID=61&id=358

http://tinyurl.com/kaiser12

David Hogberg, PhD, at the The National Center for Public Policy Research wrote an article: "Sweden's Single-Payer Health System Provides a Warning to Other Nations", accessed 1/20/10

http://www.nationalcenter.org/NPA555_Sweden_Health_Care.html

http://tinyurl.com/hogberg

M.Harrison. *"The reorientation of market-oriented reforms in Swedish health-care"* Health Policy. Vol. 50, Issue 3. Pages 219-240

Folkhemmet

Richard W. Rahn wrote another excellent article about the Sweden in Washington Times, accessed 1/15/10

http://www.washingtontimes.com/news/2004/apr/25/20040425-102740-9436r//print/

http://tinyurl.com/Rahn-Sweden1

Mammoth Entities

The sheer size of the health care industry in federal statistics, accessed 1/10/10

http://www.bls.gov/oco/cg/cgs035.htm

http://www.tinyurl.com/size-org

Government Becomes Your Kids Parent

The Guttmacher Institute country report regarding Sweden has a lot of background information and data. Some of the data is slightly older. It will explain some of the major concepts. As accessed 2/7/10

http://www.guttmacher.org/pubs/summaries/sweden_teen.pdf

A document that explains more about the concept of "youth clinics" that is written in clear favor of these clinics as: "The youth clinics are a place where young people of both sexes, from 15 – 23 years age, come for contraceptive counseling, testing and treatment for STI, abortion advice, problems at home and at school, other personal problems but also to learn more about sexual and reproductive health." You can read it in the clear understanding that the paper is in favor of government taking over your parental responsibilities and rights.

http://www.medsci.uu.se/klinbakt/stigup/Publications/ARTICLES/article%20archive/015A11.pdf

http://tinyurl.com/youthclinic

Abortion as Birth Control

Promemoria from Ostergotalands County Council regarding abortions (Swedish), accessed 1/18/10

http://tinyurl.com/ostergotland1

Ekstrand M, Larsson M, Von Essen L, Tydén T. *Swedish teenager perceptions of teenage pregnancy, abortion, sexual behavior, and contraceptive habits--a focus group study among 17-year-old female high-school students."*Acta Obstet Gynecol Scand. 2005. Oct:84 (10):980-6.

Suing the Health Care System? Forget it!

Information from the Swedish universal healthcare system regarding patient's right to compensation (English), accessed 2/7/10

http://tinyurl.com/patientsweden

Soviet-styled Redistribution

The Swede's have taken the tax enforcement to fund for redistribution to a new level. This document in English is more a war on personal equity than fair taxation. The document is from the Swedish IRS, Skatteverket, accessed 2/7/10

http://www.skatteverket.se/download/18.225c96e811ae46c823f800014872/Report_2008_1B.pdf

http://tinyurl.com/taxwar

The Swedish IRS, Skatteverket, has created a summary of the taxes collected in Sweden and what type of taxes. It is in English, accessed 2/7/10

http://www.skatteverket.se/download/18.69ef368911e1304a625800017687/10409.pdf

http://tinyurl.com/swedtaxes

Population Registry and Control

Sweden denies illegal immigrants any health care benefits, accessed 2/7/10

http://findarticles.com/p/articles/mi_kmafp/is_200805/ai_n25441395/

http://tinyurl.com/illegalinsweden

Swedish Internal Revenue Service, Skatteverket, has created a document that explains the population registry, accessed 2/7/10

http://www.skatteverket.se/download/18.b7f2d0103e5e9ecb08000127/717b03.pdf

http://tinyurl.com/popregistry

Taxes, Taxes, Taxes – And More Tax Men

IRS is likely to monitor peoples' compliance, accessed 1/10/10

http://www.foxnews.com/politics/2010/01/07/final-health-care-require-proof-insurance-tax-returns/

http://www.tinyurl.com/irshealthcare

The Heritage Foundation's freedom ranking rates fiscal freedom, in other words, taxes. Sweden rank very low as a developed country and the need for high taxes is to a degree driven by the funding of the universal health care, as accessed by 1/20/10

http://www.heritage.org/index/country/Sweden

http://tinyurl.com/heritage4

A Fox News article about Swedish tax agents chasing web cam strippers for tax compliance, just to show the extent of tax enforcement, accessed 2/7/10

http://www.foxnews.com/story/0,2933,514218,00.html

http://tinyurl.com/foxsweden

JON KALLBERG

Jon Kallberg grew up in Sweden and at an early age realized that socialism made no sense. During the 1970s, the leftist winds were in full blow through Western Europe with strong anti-sentiment against the United States. He as not even a teenager made up is mind when it comes to politics.

Jon has debated for the last thirty years in Sweden through books, articles, and speeches in defense of freedom, liberty, and the individual's rights. He has authored twelve books, written over 700 op-ed articles, and columns. He was a columnist for Sweden's largest daily newspaper, Metro, for seven years. In Sweden he uses Jan Kallberg as pen name.

During the 1980s, he traveled extensively through Soviet-occupied Eastern Europe strengthening his belief in the fundamental values that some take for granted: justice, equality and freedom of speech.

He organized a fifth of the campaign budget, that was smuggled through Soviet border controls to conservatives in occupied Estonia, providing resources for their electoral campaign, which supported the creation of Estonia's first elected government in fifty years. In the late 1980s, he traveled as a journalist through the Angolan Civil War where Cuban and Soviet troops were fighting a savage war against insurgents backed by Ronald Reagan. He is one of three that has travelled from the Caprivi Strip to the Zaire border in the midst of the war and one out of two that survived.

Jon Kallberg holds a J.D. / LL.M. from Juridicum Law School, Stockholm University, a M.A. in Political Science from University of Texas at Dallas.

He served as a reserve officer and 1st lieutenant in Sweden for sixteen years and ended his service as an Army Ranger. He joined the Swedish Armed Forces at the age of 17.

He can be reached at jk@rakapuckar.com .

9 780984 349302